Study Guide

Student Edition

~~~

Ye shall be as gods

Study Guide

Student Edition

~~~

Ye shall be as gods

Humanism and Christianity

~~~

The Battle for Supremacy in the American
Cultural Vision

Larry G. Johnson

Published by Anvil House Publishers, LLC
Owasso, Oklahoma
www.anvilhousebooks.com

Printed in the United States of America.
Cover: Whitley Graphics
Cover Photo: iStockphoto.com

ISBN: 978-0-9839716-2-7

Library of Congress Control Number for the *Ye shall be as gods*
on which this Study Guide was based: 2011916969

Contents

The Value and Purpose of the Study Guide

The purpose of writing *Ye shall be as gods* was to diagnose and illuminate the causes of the cultural disquiet that is and has been pervasive in American life for the last half century. The book provides a comprehensive overview of the source of the anger, frustration, and sense of helplessness as Americans see the Judeo-Christian ethic upon which the nation was founded come under relentless attack in the institutions of American life. The Study Guide provides a distillation of those fundamental and compelling truths that were the basis of the American cultural vision. The Study Guide will:

- Give an understanding of the tenets and tactics of humanism and the failure of the humanistic worldview to answer the basic questions of life.

- Equip Christians with definitive answers in the battle of worldviews as they work toward renewing and restoring the culture.

- Increase faith as the reader understands the Bible is the source of the infallible truth of God for all of mankind and for all time.

- Provide prescriptive remedies necessary to counteract humanism's unrelenting assault on the American cultural vision.

The Study Guide may be used by groups or individuals. The Teacher Edition provides questions and answers. The Student Edition provides questions with space to write answers. Both editions give the page numbers of the book where answers may be found to the questions posed. Sources of quotations and other reference material used in the Study Guide are not reproduced in the Study Guide. The location of these sources and reference material will be found on the pages of the book referred to in the Study Guide.

Part I – The Boomers

Introduction

1. In the last paragraph of the Introduction, what causes the author a sense of disquiet?
   (7-8)

_____

_____

_____

_____

_____

_____

_____

Chapter 1 – The Baby Boomers – Growing Up

1. What are the birth years and size for the Greatest Generation, Silent Generation, and Boomers? (10-11)

_____

_____

_____

_____

_____

_____

_____

_____

2. What are the characteristics of the three generations? (10)

_____

_____

_____

_____

_____

_____

_____

3. What shapes the consciousness of an entire generation? (11)

_____
_____
_____
_____
_____
_____
_____
_____

4. The significant shared events and formative experiences of the Boomers resulted in dramatic changes in what areas of American life? (11)

_____
_____

5. The Boomers' first two significant shared events and formative experiences were most influenced by which two men and in what areas of American life? (11)

_____
_____

6. Why was Benjamin Spock so important in forming the Boomers' worldview? (11-12, 21)

_____
_____
_____
_____
_____
_____

7. How did Spock's approach to child rearing impact the Boomer generation and those that followed? (16, 21)

_____
_____
_____
_____
_____

_____

_____

_____

_____

_____

_____

_____

_____

_____

_____

_____

8. How did Spock's approach to discipline of children differ from the traditionalists' view? (17)

_____

_____

_____

_____

_____

_____

_____

_____

_____

9. What was the ultimate impact of Spock's philosophy in raising children? (20)

_____

_____

10. What two men influenced Spock's worldview the most, and what were those influences? (21)

_____

_____

_____

_____

_____

_____
_____
_____
_____
_____
_____

11. What was the philosophy of John Dewey? (24-25)

_____
_____
_____
_____
_____
_____
_____
_____
_____
_____
_____
_____
_____

12. How did John Dewey's humanistic philosophy capture American education? (25)

_____
_____
_____
_____
_____
_____
_____
_____

Chapter 2 – Boomers – The Fifties

1. What was the Boomers' third significant shared event and formative experience and how did it become so significant? (28)

_____

_____

_____

_____

_____

_____

_____

_____

_____

_____

2. How did television impact family life? (28)

_____

_____

_____

3. What was television's impact on the larger culture outside of the home? (29)

_____

_____

_____

_____

_____

_____

_____

_____

4. What were the Boomers' fourth significant shared event and formative experience and how did that experience and event make Boomers different from other generations? (30)

5. What effect did the size of the Boomer cohort have on them? (31-32)

_____

_____

_____

_____

_____

_____

_____

_____

_____

_____

_____

6. What were the events that caused American prosperity to become the fifth significant shared event and formative experience? (32)

_____

_____

_____

_____

_____

_____

_____

_____

_____

_____

_____

7. How did this exceptionally prosperous era affect the Boomers? (32-33)

8. What was the Boomers' sixth significant shared event and formative experience and what caused it? (34)

9. List several of these technological achievements and discuss the reasons that one of those achievements is ranked as being most important. (34-36)

10. What was the attitude of many of the Boomers in the 1960s and 1970s with regard to their parents' generation and the decade of the 1950s? (37)

_____
_____
_____
_____
_____
_____
_____
_____
_____

11. How does the author rebut these charges? (37-40)

Willful authority and blind conformity_____
_____
_____
_____
_____
_____
_____
_____
_____

Materialism_____
_____
_____
_____
_____
_____
_____
_____
_____

Bigotry, racism, and repression_____
_____
_____
_____
_____

Chapter 3 – Boomers – The Sixties – Ye shall not surely die

1. Describe the origins of the worldview of the Greatest Generation. (43)

   _____

   _____

   _____

   _____

   _____

2. Although President John Kennedy was a member of the Greatest Generation and shared that generation's worldview, how did his election and the 1960s in general differ from the 1950s? (43-44)

   _____

   _____

   _____

   _____

   _____

   _____

3. What is the stereotypical image of the Boomers and why is it not descriptive of the majority of the Boomer generation? (44)

   _____

   _____

   _____

   _____

   _____

4. How were the Boomers divided with regard to lifestyles and values? (44-46)

   _____

   _____

   _____

   _____

   _____

   _____

   _____

5. What are the radical/protester achievements of the Boomer
   culture claimed by Leonard Steinhorn? (47)

6. Discuss the myth of the Boomer generation's claim to be
   responsible for all of the great social and political revolutions
   of the 1960s. (48)

7. What were the three broad currents of social and political
   change in the 1960s? (48)

8. What are the three significant areas of cultural change in the
   1960s as described by the author? Summarize each. (48-50)

11

_____
_____
_____
_____
_____
_____
_____
_____
_____
_____
_____
_____
_____
_____
_____
_____
_____
_____
_____
_____
_____
_____
_____
_____

9. Describe the status of discrimination and equality in America during the 1940s and 1950s. (51)

_____
_____
_____

10. Describe America's efforts at eliminating racial discrimination in the 1940s and 1950s. (51-52)

_____
_____
_____
_____
_____

_____

_____

_____

_____

_____

_____

_____

_____

11. What were the subtle changes in the fight for equality in the early 1960s as described by the author, and what were the causes for this new view of equality? (52)

_____

_____

_____

_____

_____

_____

_____

_____

_____

12. What were the elements that hindered the progress toward racial equality, harmony, and brotherhood as espoused in Martin Luther King's "I have a dream" speech in 1963? (52-53)

_____

_____

_____

_____

_____

_____

_____

13. Describe the fundamental difference in the approach to equality and morality between Martin Luther King and those holding the humanistic worldview. (53)

14. What was the ultimate result of the quest for equality as opposed to a quest for racial harmony and brotherhood? (54-55)

15. Describe the geo-political domino theory and its application to South Vietnam. (58-59)

_____

_____

_____

_____

16. During America's involvement in the Vietnam, one year
    stands out as the epitome of the turmoil in America during the
    1960s. Name that year and describe the events that defined the
    decade. (59)

_____

_____

_____

_____

_____

_____

_____

_____

17. What happened to the rebellious Boomers following the
    1960s? (65-66)

_____

_____

_____

_____

_____

_____

_____

Part II – Worldview

Chapter 4 – Worldview: Christianity vs. Humanism

1. Describe what is meant by "worldview." (70)

_____
_____
_____
_____
_____
_____
_____
_____

2. Why must we concern ourselves with worldview? (70)

_____
_____
_____
_____
_____
_____
_____

3. How do conflicting worldviews affect a culture? (71)

_____
_____
_____
_____
_____
_____
_____
_____
_____

4. Are all worldviews of equal value? (71-72)

_____

_____

_____

_____

_____

_____

5. How does Princeton Professor Robert George define the
   conflict of worldviews in America? (72)

_____

_____

_____

_____

_____

_____

_____

6. How do the humanists depict the combatants in the battle of
   worldviews? (72-73)

_____

_____

_____

_____

_____

_____

_____

_____

_____

7. Why do humanists present secularism as a neutral doctrine that
   deserves privileged status as the national public philosophy
   and what is the Christian's response? (73)

_____

_____

_____

_____

_____

_____

_____

_____

_____

8. In the West, why have secularists' tactics been so successful in
   its battle with the Judeo-Christian worldview? (73)

_____

_____

_____

_____

_____

_____

Chapter 5 – The Fingerprints of God

1. How is it that a perceived truth that transcends the senses and time can be understood by both the ancient philosophers and modern primitives? (78)

_____

_____

_____

_____

_____

_____

_____

_____

_____

2. Upon what must a worldview be conditioned? (78)

_____

_____

_____

_____

_____

_____

_____

_____

3. What are those things thought to be mysterious and superior, and worthy of being sought to the exclusion of everything else? (78-79)

_____

_____

_____

_____

_____

_____

_____

_____

_____

_____

_____

_____

_____

_____

_____

_____

_____

_____

4. Describe Russell Kirk's perceptions of the need for order in
    our lives and the consequences of a life lived without order.
    (79-80)

_____

_____

_____

_____

_____

_____

_____

_____

_____

_____

_____

_____

_____

_____

_____

_____

5. What are Blackstone's twin pillars of the law and why are they
    important? (80-81)

_____

_____

_____

_____

6. What is the difference between the laws of nature and laws of human nature? (82)

7. How does a society develop a collective worldview and with what must it align itself? (83-84)

8. What are the questions that every worldview or belief system must answer? (84)

_____
_____
_____
_____
_____
_____
_____
_____
_____

9. Define the following terms and their relative positions in
    American life: modernism, post-Christian and postmodernism.
    (84-85)

_____
_____
_____
_____
_____
_____
_____
_____
_____
_____
_____

10. What is the Christian worldview? (86)

_____
_____
_____
_____
_____
_____
_____
_____
_____
_____
_____

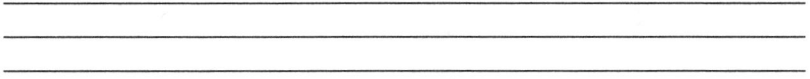

Chapter 6 – The Judeo-Christian Tradition and the Rise of Western Civilization

1. What became of Christianity at the fall of the Roman Empire in the fifth century? (88)

_____

_____

_____

_____

_____

_____

_____

_____

_____

_____

2. Under what conditions did the remnant of Christianity live after they fled to Europe from the failed Roman Empire, and how did their society develop? (88)

_____

_____

_____

_____

_____

_____

_____

_____

_____

_____

_____

_____

_____

_____

_____

_____

3. What happened to the eastern half of the Christian world following its fall to the Turks and what was the impact on Western civilization? (89)

_____

_____

_____

_____

_____

_____

_____

_____

_____

_____

4. What is Christian humanism and what was its effect on the Age of Faith? (89)

_____

_____

_____

_____

_____

_____

_____

_____

_____

_____

5. How did two thirteenth century Christian philosophers profoundly affect the course of Christianity and the Catholic Church and who were they? (89-90)

_____

_____

_____

_____

_____

_____

6. What is the nominalist doctrine and how did it further undermine the focus on realism in the fourteenth century? (90)

_____

_____

_____

7. Following the centralization of the power of the church under the papacy during the twelfth and thirteenth centuries, certain abuses occurred within the church which lasted to the beginning of the sixteenth century and coincided with the Renaissance and later Age of Enlightenment. What were these occurrences and events that would forever change the church? (90-91)

_____

_____

_____

_____

_____

_____

_____

_____

_____

_____

_____

_____

_____

_____

_____

_____

_____

_____

8. What was the result of the schism between the two great arms of the Church? (91-92)

_____

_____

_____

_____

_____

_____

_____

_____

_____

9. What was the Enlightenment, when did it occur, and what was its center? (92)

_____

_____

_____

_____

_____

_____

_____

_____

_____

_____

_____

10. Through the Enlightenment came the notion that there were no moral values that arose from fixed ideas of right and wrong. Describe this concept and its consequences. (93)

_____

_____

_____

_____

_____

_____

_____

Chapter 7 – The Renaissance and Enlightenment – Progress and Perfection – Science and Reason

1. While the Catholics and Protestants were at war, the champions of the Renaissance and Enlightenment used two weapons in their attack on faith. What were these weapons? (95)

    _____

    _____

    _____

2. How did Enlightenment philosophers use science to challenge the Christianity? (95)

    _____

    _____

    _____

    _____

    _____

    _____

    _____

    _____

    _____

3. How do humanists view Christianity and Enlightenment thought? (97)

    _____

    _____

    _____

    _____

4. The author gives three reasons for the success of humanists in promoting this perceived conflict between science and Christianity. What is the first reason? (97)

    _____

    _____

    _____

    _____

    _____

5. How do Christians view religion and science? (97)

_____
_____
_____
_____
_____
_____

6. What was the humanist objective in creating a conflict between science and religion? (97-98)

_____
_____
_____
_____
_____

7. A second reason that humanists have succeeded in creating the perceived conflict between science and religion is the belief that science has disproved Christianity and thereby reinforces the supposed gap between scientific truth and the Christian myth. What is the Christian's answer to this assertion? (98-99)

_____
_____
_____
_____
_____
_____
_____

8. The author speaks of three ways of knowing or defining reality. Humanists accept two but Christians put forward a third. Explain the three ways of determining or knowing reality. (99-100)

_____
_____
_____

29

_____
_____
_____
_____
_____
_____
_____
_____

9.   What is a third reason humanists have succeeded in creating the perceived conflict between science and Christianity? (101-102)

_____
_____
_____
_____
_____
_____
_____
_____
_____
_____
_____
_____
_____
_____
_____

10. The first weapon used by humanists in attacking faith was science. What is the second weapon and how did it arise? (103-104)

_____
_____
_____
_____
_____
_____
_____

11. What is the Christian view of reason? (105)

12. How does God help man when man has faulty reasoning? (105)

13. The author states that reason is an ally of faith. What does he mean? (106)

14. How do the Catholic and Protestant views of reason differ? (107-110)

15. If man's reason is faulty due to man's corrupted nature, of what value is reason to the Christian? (111)

Chapter 8 – Colonial American Heritage

1. What were the two pillars upon which the Founders created the American Government? (115)

_____

_____

_____

_____

2. What was the source of the American heritage of liberty? (115-116)

_____

_____

_____

_____

_____

_____

_____

3. How did the concepts of a free government through constitutionalism arise during the Middle Ages? (116-117)

_____

_____

_____

_____

_____

_____

_____

_____

_____

4. How were the traditions of English law and constitutionalism that had grown over a thousand years challenged in Britain between the beginning of the Reformation in 1517 and the Glorious Revolution of 1688? (117)

_____
_____
_____
_____
_____
_____
_____
_____
_____
_____
_____
_____
_____

5. What effect did the English kings' challenges to the traditions of English law and constitutionalism have on those fleeing England for the American colonies? (118)

_____
_____
_____
_____
_____

6. What was the primary reason the colonists came to America? (118)

_____
_____
_____

7. What is deism and to why did it not greatly influence the American colonies during the eighteen century? (120-121)

_____
_____
_____
_____
_____
_____
_____
_____

_____

_____

_____

_____

8. The author describes three reasons that illustrate the relatively inconsequential influence of deism and Enlightenment thought in the eighteenth century as a foundation for the Revolution and founding of the United States. Name and briefly describe each of those reasons. (123-126)

First_____

_____

_____

_____

_____

_____

_____

Second_____

_____

_____

_____

_____

_____

Third_____

_____

_____

_____

_____

_____

_____

_____

Chapter 9 – The American Founders and Their Beliefs

1. Although the American colonies did not exhibit a significant hierarchy of classes as was present in England, the author discusses several broad groups that comprised American colonial society. Identify these groups and movements between groups. (129-130)

_____
_____
_____
_____
_____
_____
_____
_____
_____
_____
_____
_____
_____
_____
_____
_____
_____

2. Why did both early and modern historians discount the role of religion in the Revolutionary period, and why is their view not supported by the historical record? (131-132)

_____
_____
_____
_____
_____
_____
_____
_____
_____
_____

3. What were the religious beliefs of Americans during the Revolutionary period and how did these beliefs impact the design of American government? (132)

_____

_____

_____

_____

_____

_____

_____

_____

_____

4. What were the fundamental differences between the French and American Revolutions as described by Edmund Burke and others? (133)

_____

_____

_____

_____

_____

_____

_____

_____

_____

_____

5. In drafting the Constitution, the Founders examined the two extremes of the continuum of political power and control. What were these extremes, and how did the Founders design the Constitution to avoid these extremes? (134)

_____

_____

_____

_____

_____

_____

_____

_____

_____

_____

_____

6. What was the central difficulty the Founders recognized in
   drafting the Constitution to reflect the people's law? (134-135)

_____

_____

_____

_____

_____

_____

_____

7. Explain what Constitutional liberals mean when they say the
   Constitution should be a "living document", and what are the
   dangers thereof? (136-137)

_____

_____

_____

_____

_____

_____

_____

_____

_____

_____

_____

_____

_____

_____

_____

Chapter 10 – The Roots and Rise of Modern Humanism

1. What civilization and in what period did the man-made philosophy of humanism receive significant advancement? (139)

_____

_____

_____

_____

2. How does J. M. Roberts describe the influence of the Greeks with regard to humanism? (140)

_____

_____

_____

_____

_____

_____

_____

3. What were the fundamental beliefs of Plato which stood in opposition to the humanistic Greek philosophers of the age? (141)

_____

_____

_____

_____

4. Describe the first clash between the humanistic worldview of the Greeks and that of infant Christianity in the first century AD. (145)

_____

_____

_____

_____

5. What did Thomas Aquinas believe with regard to the classical and Christian explanations of the world and what were the consequences? (148)

_____

_____

_____

_____

_____

_____

_____

6. In *The Philosophy of Humanism,* written in 1949, Dr. Corliss Lamont lists ten central propositions to describe the humanist philosophy. Summarize each. (149-150)

_____

_____

_____

_____

_____

_____

_____

_____

_____

_____

_____

_____

_____

_____

_____

_____

_____

_____

_____

_____

_____

_____

_____

_____

_____

_____

_____

_____

_____

_____

7. Briefly summarize the elements of the two basic branches of humanism as described by Lamont. (150-151)

_____

_____

_____

_____

_____

_____

_____

Chapter 11 – The "Why"—Worldviews of Humanism and Christianity

1. The author states that there are three ways in which man can obtain clues as to why God created the universe and mankind. What are these three ways? (157)

_____

_____

_____

_____

_____

2. How is man's need for relationships a reflection of the character of God? (157-158)

_____

_____

_____

_____

_____

_____

3. In describing man's chief end as glorifying God by communing with God forever, the author discusses the reason God gave man a free will. Discuss that reason. (158)

_____

_____

_____

_____

_____

_____

_____

4. What was the penalty for rejection of God? (158)

_____

_____

_____

_____
_____
_____
_____
_____
_____
_____
_____

5. What are the permanent things, universal truths that point to the laws which guide the universe, nature, and human nature and what is their connection to the biblical revelation? (159)

_____
_____
_____
_____
_____
_____
_____
_____
_____
_____
_____

6. When humanists attempt to discredit Christianity and belief in an omnipotent, benevolent, and personal God by saying that the immensity of the universe could only be known to modern man, how does the Christian respond? (161)

_____
_____
_____
_____
_____
_____
_____
_____

7. How does the humanist view the age of the universe? (161)

_____

_____

_____

_____

_____

_____

_____

_____

_____

_____

_____

8. Humanists point to the enormous time spans and eternally existing nature of the cosmos as evidence that speaks against Christianity. How does the Christian respond? (161-162)

_____

_____

_____

_____

_____

_____

9. With regard to the creation of the universe, what is the scientific evidence that points to the existence of God and the purposeful design of the world for man? (163-164)

_____

_____

_____

_____

_____

_____

_____

_____

_____

_____

10. With regard to the connection between the mind and physical body, the humanists hold to the monistic theory while Christians hold to the dualistic theory. Describe the two theories. (166)

Part III – Worldview

1. What was the secular revolution that began about 1870 as described by Christian Smith? (169)

_____

_____

_____

_____

_____

2. What was the consequence of the secular revolution? (169)

_____

_____

_____

_____

Chapter 12 – Religion – The Power of Religion in American History

1. Richard Weaver called man a special creature with two selves. What did he mean?
   (171-172)

_____

_____

_____

_____

_____

_____

_____

_____

2. How does the author describe religion and the power thereof? (172-173)

_____

_____

_____

_____

3. What is the humanists' view of religion and its origin? (173)

4. Are all religions of equal value or worth? (174)

5. What weapons do humanists use to undermine Christianity and what is the Christian's response? (174)

6. How do humanists attempt to prove the falsity of the Bible and how should the Christian respond? (175-176)

_____

_____

_____

_____

_____

_____

_____

_____

_____

_____

_____

7. What was the purpose of the biblical revelation and in what manner was it presented? (176)

_____

_____

_____

_____

_____

_____

_____

_____

_____

_____

8. Define "inerrant" and "literal" as applied to the Bible. How do humanists use these terms to in their attempts to discredit the Bible, and what is the Christian response? (177)

_____

_____

_____

_____

_____

_____

_____

_____

9. If the infallibility of the Bible is derived from the belief that the words of the Scripture are God breathed (written by human hands but under the inspiration of God), how does the Christian defend the Bible's infallibility when the humanists attempt to undermine the authority of the Scripture by pointing to the numerous translations of the Bible through the centuries, and therefore claim the Bible can't be accurate as that of the original versions? (180)

Chapter 13 – Religion in the Public Arena – Mention Jesus Christ and "…all hell breaks loose"

1. How does the Christian respond when someone says that religion is such a deeply personal issue it is wrong to discuss what another person should believe? (182)

_____
_____
_____
_____
_____
_____
_____
_____
_____
_____
_____
_____
_____
_____

2. How does the Christian respond to the humanist that chastises Christians for presuming the Christian faith is superior to other faiths when all faiths lead to the same God? (183-184)

_____
_____
_____
_____
_____
_____
_____
_____
_____
_____
_____
_____

3. How and why do humanists promote the dualism of faith and society? (184)

4. Under what banner do Humanists promote the dualism of faith and society? (184-185)

5. When Tocqueville arrived in the United States in 1830, he was struck by the religious atmosphere which he attributed to the separation of church and state. How was that separation of church and state different from the humanists' "wall of separation" used to drive Christianity from the public square? (185)

6. How do we reconcile Tocqueville's "separation of church and state" with his "reign of the spirit of religion over the land"? (186-187)

7. Given that America is a nation of immigrants, compare and contrast the moral suasion of the Christian faith with the leveling practices of the humanistic philosophy in bringing unity and cohesion to the nation. (188)

8. What is the premise behind the humanists' leveling practice of multiculturalism? (189)

9. What is the essence of multiculturalism? (190)

10. Why has the growth of Christianity around the world been so successful given that it is supposedly forcing various groups into a cultural straitjacket? (191)

_____
_____
_____
_____
_____
_____
_____
_____
_____

11. Summarize what Richard Weaver believed regarding how culture develops, how it operates, and what must it do to survive. (192-193)

How culture develops _____
_____
_____
_____
_____
_____
_____

How culture operates_____
_____
_____
_____
_____
_____
_____

How cultures fail_____
_____
_____
_____

12. How does one reconcile tolerance in society and a culture's need for exclusivity? (193)

_____

_____

_____

_____

_____

_____

_____

_____

_____

_____

_____

13. At what point must a pluralistic society suspend tolerance and act in opposition to a rival culture? (194)

_____

_____

_____

_____

14. Compare and contrast the Christian and humanist basis for morality. (195-196)

_____

_____

_____

_____

_____

_____

_____

_____

_____

_____

_____

_____

Chapter 14 – Government – "…America is not a Christian nation"

1. If President Obama does not consider America a Christian nation, Jewish nation, or a Muslim nation, what values does he see as guiding the nation? (200)

_____

_____

_____

2. How does the author counter President Obama's assertion that we are guided by secular values? (200)

_____

_____

_____

_____

3. In his 2006 speech regarding his vision for America, what does President Obama believe that democracy demands of the religiously motivated and what is his justification for his belief? (201)

_____

_____

_____

_____

_____

_____

_____

_____

_____

_____

_____

_____

4. How do secular humanists use Thomas Jefferson's "wall of separation between church and state" to drive Christianity from the institutions of American life? (202-204)

5. What is the correct interpretation of the establishment clause and Jefferson's "wall of separation"? (202-203, 202n-203n)

6. What is the evidence that supports the fact that the United States was founded upon Christian principles? (206)

7. In the Supreme Court case, *Holy Trinity v. United States, 1892*, what was the court's conclusion with regard to the obligation to govern by Christian principles and to oppose enactment and enforcement of laws contrary to those principles? (208)

8. What is the Christian's answer to the secularist who says that the principles upon which the nation is governed should be religion neutral as only a secular worldview can provide, i.e., a safe, religion free alternative? (209-210)

9. What did William Blackstone believe with regard to the laws of society? (211)

Chapter 15 – Government – Liberalism and Progressivism in America

1. What was the political legacy of the Enlightenment and how does it differ from the Christian worldview? (213)

_____
_____
_____
_____
_____
_____
_____
_____

2. Describe the skeptical revolutionary cultural tradition that emanated from the age of Enlightenment? (213)

_____
_____
_____
_____
_____

3. As the secularization of American society occurred between 1870 and 1930, how did evangelical Protestant Christianity respond? (214)

_____
_____
_____
_____
_____
_____
_____
_____
_____
_____
_____

4. What is the difference between the liberalism at the founding of the United States and the creation of its Constitution and that of contemporary liberalism? (214)

_____

_____

_____

_____

_____

_____

_____

_____

_____

5. What are the two supports upon which the contemporary liberal rests? (24-215)

_____

_____

_____

_____

_____

_____

_____

6. Why does liberalism's concern for the individual (dignity of the individual, freedom of speech, and equal rights before the law) divorced from the Judeo-Christian ethic rest on a fallacy? (215)

_____

_____

_____

7. According to Russell Kirk, liberalism contains four universal articles of faith. Summarize each of these. (214-215)

Affectation of Change _____

_____

_____

Exaltation of the individual_____

_____

_____

_____

_____

Discard tradition and its foundations_____

_____

_____

_____

_____

Progress_____

_____

_____

_____

_____

8. How is conservatism both different from and not the opposite of liberalism? (216)

_____

_____

_____

_____

_____

_____

_____

_____

_____

9. What is the foundational concept underpinning liberalism and ultimately humanism? (217)

_____

_____

_____

_____

10. Contrast a liberal's progressivism and a conservative's prescription for order in society? (218-219)

_____

_____

_____

_____

_____

_____

_____

_____

_____

_____

11. How does the humanists' exaltation of the dignity and preciousness of the individual (5th principle of Humanist Manifesto II) conflict with the humanist commitment to some form of the greatest-happiness-for-the-greatest-number principle which they consider the highest moral obligation to humanity as a whole? (220-221)

_____

_____

_____

_____

_____

_____

_____

_____

_____

12. How do those holding the Judeo-Christian ethic view the individual? (222)

_____

_____

_____

_____

_____

_____

_____

_____

_____

_____

_____

13. According to Richard Weaver, what are the three ways
humanists attempt to devalue or demote man? (223)

Insignificance of man _____

_____

_____

_____

_____

Diminished worth of man _____

_____

_____

_____

Loss of free will _____

_____

_____

_____

_____

14. What has been the definition of freedom through the ages and
why does man choose to place some limits on that freedom?
(223-224)

_____

_____

_____

_____

_____

15. Compare and contrast the biblical and humanist views of freedom. (224-225)

16. Define democracy—what it is and what it is not. (226-227)

17. How have humanists redefined democracy to further their humanistic goals for society? (227)

_____
_____
_____
_____
_____
_____
_____
_____
_____
_____
_____
_____
_____
_____
_____
_____

18. What is the difference between equality and fraternity as it relates to a culture? (229)

_____
_____
_____
_____
_____
_____
_____
_____
_____
_____

19. Why will the humanist's ideal of equality never achieve social harmony? (229-230)

_____
_____
_____
_____
_____

_____
_____
_____
_____
_____
_____
_____
_____
_____
_____

20. What was the fallacy of the eighteenth century philosophers' democratic ideas of human equality? (230-231)

_____
_____
_____
_____
_____
_____
_____
_____
_____

21. What was the equality proposed by John Adams and the other founders? (231-232)

_____
_____
_____
_____

22. Having failed to provide equality of income through political equality, what were the new demands of humanists and what were the tactics used to achieve their goals? (232-233)

_____
_____
_____
_____

23. Describe the concept of justice and its connection to order and freedom. (233-235)

_____

_____

_____

_____

_____

_____

_____

_____

_____

_____

_____

_____

_____

_____

_____

_____

24. How have humanists redefined justice to fit their worldview? (234)

_____

_____

_____

_____

_____

_____

_____

_____

Chapter 16 – Government – Humanism and the Rise of Socialism

1. How are the humanist philosophy and socialism linked? (237-238)

_____

_____

_____

_____

_____

_____

_____

_____

_____

2. Socialism as a foundation for modern collectivist governments originated when and where, and what was the underlying fallacy upon which it was based? (238-239)

_____

_____

_____

_____

_____

_____

_____

_____

_____

_____

_____

3. What was the essence of the Communist Manifesto written by Marx and Engels in 1848? (241)

_____

_____

_____

_____

_____

_____

_____

4. What does the author suggest is the true end result of the socialist's lofty and altruistic goals of justice, equality, and security? (242)

_____

_____

_____

_____

5. According to Hayek, how do the levelers sell socialism when it implicitly requires a limit on the strongest political motive—the urge for freedom? (242)

_____

_____

_____

_____

_____

_____

_____

6. In practical terms, what is the end result of the imposition on society of this new freedom? (243)

_____

_____

_____

_____

_____

7. Describe the beginnings of the social gospel movement in the United States and the end result thereof. (243-244)

_____

_____

_____

_____

_____

_____

_____

_____

_____

_____

_____

_____

_____

8. How does Richard Weaver describe the humanists' view of property and what is his response thereto? (248)

_____

_____

_____

_____

_____

_____

_____

_____

_____

_____

_____

_____

9. How did the Supreme Court's liberal interpretation in 1936 of the "general welfare" clause of the Constitution encroach on fundamental property rights? (249)

_____

_____

_____

_____

_____

_____

_____

_____

10. How does Charles Murray describe transformation of a free society into a socialistic society with massive government intrusion into almost every aspect of an individual's life and the end result thereof? (257-258)

_____

_____

_____

_____

_____

_____

_____

_____

_____

_____

_____

Chapter 17 – Science – Naturalistic Evolution

1. What is naturalism? (259)

_____

_____

_____

_____

_____

_____

_____

2. Describe Charles Darwin's theory of evolution and the impact thereof. (260-261)

_____

_____

_____

_____

_____

_____

_____

_____

_____

_____

_____

_____

3. How do evolutionists dismiss the extreme improbabilities of life beginning through _undirected_ natural causes and why is their explanation unacceptable? (261-262)

_____

_____

_____

_____

_____

4. Describe the theory of theistic evolution in which evolution is supposed to be God-governed but attempts to remain compatible with Darwinian evolution on scientific matters. What is the fallacy thereof? (262)

_____
_____
_____
_____
_____
_____
_____
_____
_____

5. What is the difference between macroevolution and microevolution? (263)

_____
_____
_____
_____
_____
_____
_____

6. How does the fossil record fail to support Darwin's theory of evolution?

_____
_____
_____
_____
_____
_____
_____
_____

7. How do defenders of Darwin's theory use punctuated equilibrium to explain the lack of a fossil record? (265-266)

8. What is neo-Darwinism? (267)

9. Do mutations in DNA's genetic code support Neo-Darwinists reliance on random mutation and natural selection as the primary mechanism for evolution? (268)

10. What is the concept of "irreducible complexity" and how does it pose significant problems for evolutionary theory? (269-270)

11. Given the mounting difficulties in the defense of naturalistic evolution, why is there such a massive and fierce defense of naturalistic evolution as "accepted fact"? (273)

12. How does Darwin's accepted fact of evolution differ from the accepted fact of evolution by modern day evolutionists? (274)

Chapter 18 – Human Sciences and the Secularization of America

1. In the study and understanding of human nature, why has there been so little progress in sociology and psychology? (278)

_____

_____

_____

_____

_____

_____

_____

_____

_____

2. During the last three decades of the 1800s, what was the impact of social Darwinism's capture of academia and mainstream religion through the social gospel movement? (279)

_____

_____

_____

_____

_____

_____

_____

_____

_____

3. How did the champions of human sciences (psychology and sociology) such as John Dewey view the physical and human sciences? (280)

_____

_____

_____

_____

_____

4. How did Keith Meador describe the result of mainline Protestantism's choice not to fight but to compromise, accommodate, and acquiesce to the secularizing aspects of social Darwinism? (281)

5. Why have psychologists failed for over a hundred years to gain a clear understanding of human nature? (284)

6. What is the naturalistic sociologist's understanding of human behavior and the patterns of relationships by which people are connected in society, social institutions, and social relationships? (285)

7. Why do the views of naturalistic sociology and humanistic sociology fail to adequately describe human nature? (286)

_____

_____

_____

_____

_____

_____

8. What is scientism and its tenets of belief? (287)

_____

_____

_____

_____

_____

_____

_____

_____

_____

_____

_____

_____

Chapter 19 – American Education

1. How does the author view education and instruction as being different? (289)

_____

_____

_____

_____

_____

_____

_____

2. What does the author believe to be the dominant conflict in American education for the last one hundred years? (289)

_____

_____

_____

3. Summarize eight aims of progressive education that Richard Weaver identifies as fundamentally different and in conflict with the core teachings and traditions of Western civilization as defined by the Judeo-Christian heritage? (289-290)

_____

_____

_____

_____

_____

_____

_____

_____

_____

_____

_____

_____

_____

_____

_____
_____
_____
_____
_____
_____
_____
_____
_____

4. How did higher education in North America move from an unequivocally Christian enterprise in the late nineteenth century to a monolithic secular progressive education establishment in the last half of the twentieth century? (291)

_____
_____
_____
_____
_____
_____
_____
_____
_____
_____
_____
_____
_____
_____
_____
_____

5. What is meant by the progressives' emphasis on child-centeredness in education?
    (293-294)

_____
_____
_____
_____

6. What are the two reasons given by Craig Gay for the rapid and comprehensive secularization of American education in the twentieth century? (294-295)

7. What is the Uncurriculum that Rob Koons believes prevails at most colleges and universities? (300)

8. Describe the structure of a liberal education that stands in opposition to the scatter-shot approach of the Uncurriculum. (300)

9. What are the consequences of abandoning a liberal education for the Uncurriculum? (301)

Chapter 20 – American Family – Marriage and Family

1. How does the author describe the hierarchical nature of relationships in the Christian worldview? (305)

_____

_____

_____

_____

_____

_____

_____

_____

2. What is meant by humanistic egalitarianism? (306)

_____

_____

_____

_____

3. How does the author describe the equalitarian nature of relationships in the humanistic worldview? (306)

_____

_____

_____

_____

_____

_____

_____

4. What are the consequences of modern society's loss of hierarchy? (305-306)

_____

_____

_____

_____

_____

5. Describe fraternity/brotherhood and its importance to society. (306-307)

_____

_____

_____

_____

_____

_____

_____

_____

_____

6. Describe the family structure and its place in the world. (307-308)

_____

_____

_____

_____

_____

_____

_____

_____

7. How does the author describe the highest form of the modern nuclear family? (309)

_____

_____

_____

_____

8. How has marriage remained a cultural universal while being changed and shaped over man's history? (310)

9. How do the cultural universals of marriage and family aid society? (310-311)

10. How did Christianity elevate the status of women in society? (311-312)

_____
_____
_____
_____
_____
_____
_____
_____
_____
_____

11. Why has marriage between a man and woman been such a solemn and ritualistic occasion throughout history? (312)

_____
_____
_____
_____
_____
_____
_____

12. What is the view of marriage as a contractual relationship? (313)

_____
_____
_____
_____
_____
_____
_____
_____

13. What is the view of marriage as a covenant relationship? (314)

_____
_____
_____
_____

14. How does the humanist worldview as described in *Humanist Manifesto II* conflict with the concept of covenant marriage? (314-315)

15. What are the fruits of the ascending humanist worldview since the 1960s with regard to marriage and family? (319)

Chapter 21 – American Family – Feminism and the Roles of Men and Women

1. Describe Stephanie Coontz's role characterization of the male breadwinner/full-time housewife marriages. (323)

_____
_____
_____
_____
_____
_____
_____
_____
_____
_____

2. What was the general view of the roles of husbands and wives throughout history? (323)

_____
_____
_____
_____
_____
_____
_____
_____
_____
_____

3. How and when did the roles of husband and wife emerge as society was transformed from a barter to a wage-based economy? (324)

_____
_____
_____
_____
_____

_____

_____

_____

_____

_____

_____

_____

_____

_____

_____

_____

_____

4. How has the humanist worldview of marriage and sexuality undermined the traditional roles of men and women? (326)

_____

_____

_____

_____

_____

_____

_____

_____

5. How did the Industrial Revolution impact American society and ultimately the status of women? (327)

_____

_____

_____

_____

_____

_____

_____

_____

_____

_____

6. With regard to the status of women, what was the agenda for the utopians and religious perfectionists and how was it to be achieved? (327)

7. How did Margaret Sanger package her goals of radical socialism and sexual liberation so that it would be readily accepted in the United States? (330-331)

8. As Nazi atrocities became known during World War II, how did Sanger overcome her close association with German scientists who designed Nazi Germany's "race purification" plan; her endorsement of early Reich euthanasia, sterilization, abortion, and infanticide programs; and the articles in her *Birth Control Review* that closely paralleled Nazi Aryan-White Supremacist propaganda? (331)

9. How did Betty Friedan and other feminists of the early 1960s and 1970s hope to change society with regard to women and families (as described in the National Organization of Women's Statement of Purpose)? (333-334)

10. Regarding marriage, what have been the consequences to America as the humanist philosophy of feminists (such as Betty Friedan) has been embraced by large portions of society? (334)

11. Why is the Judeo-Christian worldview with regard to marriage superior to the humanist worldview of the feminists of the 1960s and 1970s? (334)

93

12. Why is marriage central to the overall well-being of children and why is the humanistic worldview so destructive to that well-being? (336)

_____

_____

_____

_____

_____

_____

_____

_____

_____

_____

13. According to Waite and Gallaher, what gives marriage and family centrality and power within the universal social institutions? (338)

_____

_____

_____

_____

_____

_____

_____

Chapter 22 – American Family – Abortion

1. Why is it that the contrary understanding of life and its origin are at the root of the division between humanist and Christian worldviews? (341-342)

_____

_____

_____

_____

_____

_____

_____

_____

_____

_____

2. How did the rise of Christianity create a basic change in the world with regard to unborn and infant children? (342-343)

_____

_____

_____

_____

_____

_____

_____

_____

_____

_____

_____

_____

3. How do humanists separate the decisions of life from God? (343-344)

_____

_____

_____

_____

4. How do humanists soften the picture or divert attention from the horror of abortion? (344)

5. Upon what legal arguments did the Supreme Court's majority opinion rely in the Roe v. Wade decision to allow abortion? (347)

6. How did the Supreme Court's majority opinion respond to the contention of those opposed to abortion that "life begins at conception and is present throughout pregnancy…" and what is the fallacy of the court's majority opinion? (347-348)

7. How do abortionists' arguments that life does not begin until birth fail? (348-349)

8. What has been the effect of the Supreme Court's 1973 Roe v. Wade legalization of abortion decision on other life issues? (350-351)

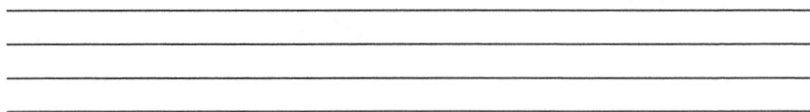

Chapter 23 – American Family – Homosexuality

1. What is the biblical position with regard to homosexuality?

_____

_____

_____

_____

_____

_____

_____

_____

_____

_____

_____

_____

2. What impact does homosexuality have on society, and how do those that support homosexuality diminish marriage and the elevate homosexuality? (354)

_____

_____

_____

_____

_____

_____

_____

_____

_____

_____

_____

_____

_____

3. What are the two general conceptions of marriage in society, and which of the two is supported by the proponents of homosexuality? (354-355)

_____
_____
_____
_____
_____
_____
_____
_____
_____
_____
_____
_____

4. What is the humanist's argument that homosexuals should be allowed to marry? (355)

_____
_____
_____
_____
_____
_____

5. What is the Judeo-Christian worldview's answer to the humanist with regard homosexuals being allowed to marry? (355-356)

_____
_____
_____
_____
_____
_____
_____

_____

_____

_____

_____

_____

_____

_____

_____

6. How do proponents of the homosexual agenda attempt to gain the moral high ground with their arguments? (356-357)

_____

_____

_____

_____

_____

_____

_____

_____

_____

7. With regard the humanist/homosexual agenda of normalization, validation, legitimation, and endorsement, what is the answer from the Judeo-Christian worldview? (357)

_____

_____

_____

_____

_____

8. Then what should be the attitude be toward the homosexual if one holds the Judeo-Christian worldview? (357)

_____

_____

_____

_____

_____

101

9. How have the proponents of homosexuality used the judicial system to further their agenda? (358)

_____
_____
_____
_____
_____
_____
_____
_____
_____
_____
_____

10. Why have many mainstream Christian churches linked themselves to the humanistic worldview with regard to their affinity for the cause of homosexuality? (360)

_____
_____
_____
_____
_____
_____
_____

11. How does one holding the Judeo-Christian worldview answer proponents of homosexuality who cite various scientific studies that indicate sexual orientation is a matter of genetics, i.e., sexual orientation is involuntary, immutable, and rooted in nature"? (361)

_____
_____
_____
_____

Chapter 24 – Popular Culture

1. What is popular culture and its connection to a society's central cultural vision? (367)

_____
_____
_____
_____
_____
_____
_____
_____
_____
_____
_____

2. How is popular culture shaped and what are the two greatest forces that influence popular culture? (367-368)

_____
_____
_____
_____
_____

3. What is the classical understanding of the purpose of art? (368)

_____
_____
_____
_____
_____
_____

4. How was the classical view of art undermined? (368-369)

5. Describe the humanistic influence on art and how it captured the arts from the classical view. (369-370)

6. Summarize the differences between the humanistic and Christian worldviews with regard to the arts. (370)

7. What is the relationship between mass media and popular
    culture, and to which worldview does mass media have a
    tendency to lean towards (humanistic or Judeo-Christian)?
    (370)

_____

_____

_____

_____

_____

8. What is the first source of the secular and humanistic
    tendencies of mass media? Briefly describe. (373)

_____

_____

_____

_____

_____

_____

_____

_____

_____

_____

_____

_____

9. What the second source of the secular and humanistic
    tendencies of mass media? Briefly describe. (374)

_____

_____

_____

10. What are the three components of mass media? (375)

11. What was Robert Bork's assessment of popular entertainment in America? (375)

12. How does advertising promote the humanistic worldview in popular culture? (376)

13. How does the flood of information available in modern society undermine the Judeo-Christian worldview? (378)

14. What is the first of two means whereby secular humanists attempt explain and defend popular culture from being a source of the decay in America life and what is the response from someone holding the Judeo-Christian worldview? (380)

_____

_____

_____

_____

_____

15. What is the second of two means whereby secular humanists attempt explain and defend popular culture from being a source of the decay in American life and what is the response from someone holding the Judeo-Christian worldview? (380-381)

_____

_____

_____

_____

_____

_____

_____

_____

_____

_____

_____

_____

_____

_____

_____

Part IV – Ye shall be as gods – Summary, Status, and Direction

Chapter 25 – Differences between Christian and Humanist Worldviews – A Summary

1. What is this book about? (385)

_____
_____
_____
_____
_____

2. What is the difference in the Christian and humanist worldviews with regard to God and creation? (385)

_____
_____
_____
_____
_____
_____
_____

3. What is the difference in the Christian and humanist worldviews with regard to man's purpose? (386)

_____
_____
_____
_____
_____
_____
_____
_____

4. What is the difference in the Christian and humanist worldviews with regard to man's creation and free will? (386)

_____

_____

_____

_____

_____

_____

_____

_____

_____

_____

5. What is the difference in the Christian and humanist
   worldviews with regard to man's nature? (387)

_____

_____

_____

_____

_____

_____

_____

_____

6. What is the difference in the Christian and humanist
   worldviews with regard to man's position and destiny? (387-
   388)

_____

_____

_____

_____

_____

_____

_____

_____

_____

_____

7. What is the difference in the Christian and humanist worldviews with regard to man's relationship to man? (389)

_____
_____
_____
_____
_____
_____
_____
_____

8. What is the difference in the Christian and humanist worldviews with regard to man as an individual? (389)

_____
_____
_____
_____
_____
_____
_____
_____
_____

9. What is the difference in the Christian and humanist worldviews with regard to societal organization and governments? (389-390)

_____
_____
_____
_____
_____
_____
_____

10. What is the difference between the Christian and humanist worldviews with regard to religion? (390-391)

_____

_____

_____

_____

_____

_____

_____

_____

11. What is the difference between the Christian and humanist worldviews with regard to marriage and family? (391)

_____

_____

_____

_____

_____

_____

_____

_____

_____

_____

12. What means have humanists used to dislodge the Judeo-Christian worldview as the central vision of American culture? (392)

_____

_____

_____

_____

_____

_____

_____

_____

_____

13. What is the difference in Christian and humanist worldviews with regard to the meaning of truth? (392-393)

_____

_____

_____

_____

_____

_____

_____

_____

_____

_____

_____

_____

14. What is the difference between the Christian and humanist worldviews with regard to the meaning of freedom? (393)

_____

_____

_____

_____

15. What is the difference between the Christian and humanist worldviews with regard to the meaning of democracy? (394)

16. What is the difference between the Christian and humanist worldviews with regard to the meaning of equality? (395)

114

_____

_____

_____

_____

_____

_____

17. What is the difference in the Christian and humanist
worldviews with regard to the meaning of justice? (396)

_____

_____

_____

_____

_____

_____

_____

_____

_____

_____

_____

18. What is the difference between the Christian and humanist
worldviews with regard to the meaning of multiculturalism?
(396-397)

_____

_____

_____

_____

_____

_____

_____

_____

_____

_____

_____

_____

19. What is the difference between the Christian and humanist worldviews with regard to the meaning of diversity? (397-398)

20. What is the difference between the Christian and humanist worldviews with regard to the meaning of tolerance? (398)

21. What is the difference between the Christian and humanist worldviews with regard to the meaning of pluralism? (399)

Chapter 26 – Christianity and Humanism – Endgame in America

1. How do cultures arise as a result of man seeing himself as a special being? (401-402)

_____

_____

_____

_____

_____

_____

_____

_____

_____

_____

2. According to Richard Weaver, what are the elements that a culture requires? (402)

_____

_____

_____

_____

3. What were the colonists' and Founders' sources upon which they relied in creating the American central cultural vision upon which the nation was founded? (402)

_____

_____

_____

_____

_____

_____

_____

_____

4. What was one of the Founders' greatest concerns when creating a government and how did they address their concerns? (403)

_____

_____

_____

_____

_____

_____

_____

_____

5. According to the author, what are some of the time-tested truths within the American central cultural vision that humanists attempt to destroy and by what means? (403)

_____

_____

_____

_____

_____

_____

_____

_____

_____

6. How does the author distinguish between the permanence of the Judeo-Christian worldview and the endangered American cultural vision of the colonists and Founders? (404)

_____

_____

_____

_____

_____

_____

7. What are the three reasons the author lists as to why the Founder's central cultural vision is in danger of removal? (404-405)

8. How does the author describe the moral and intellectual bankruptcy of humanism in American culture? (406-407)

9. In the political and economic arena, what must be done to recapture America's central cultural vision? (407)

10. Although the prescriptions in political and economic areas are important, what does the author say is most important for combating the cancer of humanism that has invaded the American cultural vision? (408)

_____
_____
_____
_____
_____
_____
_____
_____

11. What must happen in America for this order to be achieved? (408)

_____
_____
_____
_____
_____
_____
_____
_____
_____
_____
_____

12. What was the common theme or condition in America preceding each of the three major spiritual renewals during the nation's history and what was the common element that brought about the renewals? (408-413)

_____
_____
_____
_____
_____

13. What is the ultimate solution for restoration of the Judeo-Christian central cultural vision of America's Founders? (414)